CONTENTS

Abbreviations **m** stands for metres • **ft** stands for feet • **in** stands for inches • **dB** stands for decibels • **km** stands for kilometres

The biggest bang

It's early afternoon, on 27 August 1883. Two friends are talking in Perth, Western Australia. "What was that loud bang?" asked one, "Sounded like an island exploding." Correct!

The explosion was Krakatoa, an island volcano between Sumatra and Java, in Southeast Asia. It didn't just erupt like an ordinary volcano, pouring out red-hot runny rock, ash and fumes. The whole island exploded, blowing itself apart. It set off giant waves, destroyed hundreds of villages and towns, and killed over 30,000 people.

The sound of Krakatoa's eruption was so loud that people thousands of kilometres away heard it.

Krakatoa's place in the world

0   250   500 miles
0   1000 km

South China Sea

Sumatra

Borneo

INDONESIA

Krakatoa

Java

INDIAN OCEAN

TSUNAMIS

The noise spread out from the source in all directions.

Rodriques
4,900 km (3,000 miles)

Western Australia,
3,200 km
(2,000 miles)

The blast was not only deadly, it was deafening. The noise was louder and carried further than any other sound ever recorded. What are the most earsplitting noises today? Let's find out!

Huge 30-m (100-ft) high **tsunamis** raced across the ocean.

tsunamis huge waves set off by an earthquake or explosion

EXTREME!

Earsplitters!

The World's Loudest Noises

Steve Parker

A & C Black • London

Produced for A & C Black by
Monkey Puzzle Media Ltd
48 York Avenue
Hove BN3 1PJ, UK

Published by A & C Black Publishers Limited
36 Soho Square, London W1D 3QY

Paperback published 2009
First published 2008

ISBN 978-1-4081-0024-0 (hardback)
ISBN 978-1-4081-0097-4 (paperback)

A CIP catalogue record for this book is available
from the British Library.

Editor: Polly Goodman
Design: Mayer Media Ltd
Picture research: Shelley Noronha
Series consultant: Jane Turner

This book is produced using paper that is made
from wood grown in managed, sustainable forests.
It is natural, renewable and recyclable. The logging
and manufacturing processes conform to the
environmental regulations of the country of origin.

Printed in China by C & C Offset Printing Co., Ltd

Picture acknowledgements
Alamy p. 22 (Digital Vision); Corbis pp. 14 (Visuals
Unlimited), 16 (Julian Smith), 19 (Roger Ressmeyer),
21 (Jean-Yves Ruszniewski/TempSport), 25 (DLILLC);
Getty Images pp. 1, 5 (Hulton Archive), 8 (AFP), 9,
10 (Andy Williams), 11, 12 top left (Flip Nicklin),
17, 23 inset, 24 (Michael Durham), 28 (Digital
Vision), 29 (Digital Vision); iStockphoto pp. 23 main
image, 27 (Kristian Septimus Krogh); Photolibrary.com
pp. 7 (Fact Fact/Mauritius Images), 12–13 (David
B Fleetham/OSF); Ronald Grant Archive p. 18
(Paramount Pictures); Science Photo Library pp. 6
(US Air Force), 15 (CC, ISM), 20 (Jean Abitbol, ISM),
26 (Alain Pol, ISM). Artwork on p. 4 by Martin
Darlison at Encompass Graphics.

The front cover shows a helicopter flying past
exploding buildings on a movie set (Getty Images/
Pete Turner).

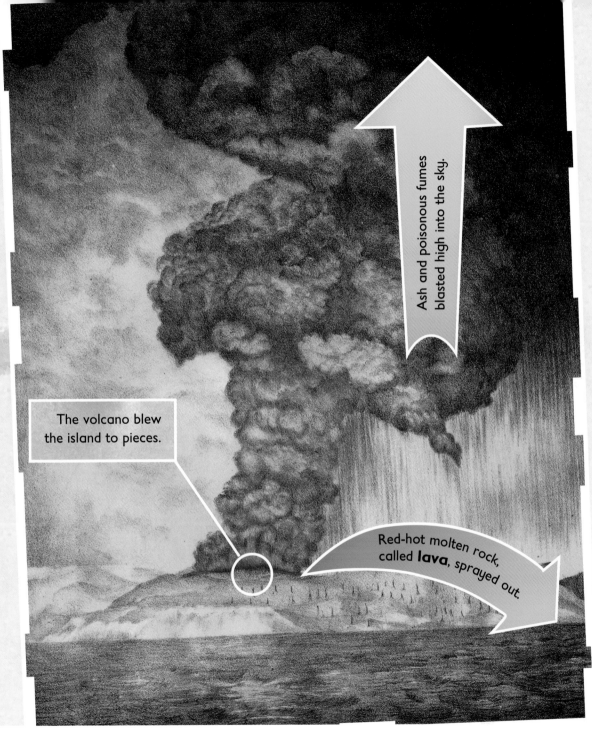

Ash and poisonous fumes blasted high into the sky.

The volcano blew the island to pieces.

Red-hot molten rock, called **lava**, sprayed out.

lava rock so hot it melts

Noisiest race on Earth

Have you ever been in a place where it's so loud, you can't hear yourself speak? Try standing near the start of a dragster race – it's the world's fastest, loudest motorsport.

From a standing start, dragsters race to the finish line a quarter of a mile (400 metres) away. They blast past the line at over 500 kilometres per hour (311 miles per hour), and produce more noise than any other sports machine.

Loudness is measured in **decibels**, or dB. An ordinary car's engine is 60–70 dB. A dragster's can be up to 150 dB. If a noise that loud lasts more than a few seconds, it could be really earsplitting and damage your hearing.

How many dBs?

Here are the decibel (dB) levels of some common sounds. Look for more over the following pages.

Whisper	20 dB
Normal speech	60 dB
Vacuum cleaner	80 dB
Road drill	100 dB

A road drill is so loud and shakes so hard that ear and hand protection is essential.

decibels unit used to measure sound's loudness or intensity

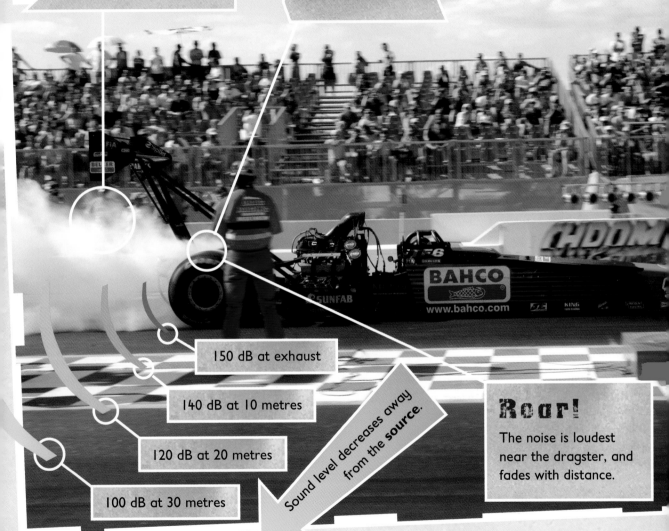

Blast!

Gases blasting out of the exhaust make the air **vibrate** and produce sound.

Shake!

The main sound comes from the exhaust.

As the dragster roars off, the start official wears very good ear protection!

150 dB at exhaust

140 dB at 10 metres

120 dB at 20 metres

100 dB at 30 metres

Sound level decreases away from the **source**.

Roar!

The noise is loudest near the dragster, and fades with distance.

vibrate to shake quickly backwards and forwards   **source** where something comes from

Let's rock!

In the giant stadium, shadowy figures are on stage. The huge loudspeakers click and hum. The spotlight shines on the guitarist. He shouts "Hello Wembley!" and blasts out an earth-shattering **KERRANG** on his guitar!

Some of the biggest sounds come from enormous loudspeakers at music events. Each loudspeaker has a cone-shaped part called a **diaphragm**. As the diaphragm vibrates, it pushes the air backwards and forwards around it, forming sound waves. The taller the sound waves, the more air they move. This means more decibels, so the sound is louder.

Loudspeakers change electrical signals into sound waves. A microphone does the opposite, turning sound waves into electrical signals, which then travel as radio waves to the amplifiers.

Heavy rock is one of the loudest music events — as played by Lemmy of the band Motorhead.

diaphragm   cone-shaped part of a loudspeaker that makes sound waves

The diaphragm in the loudspeaker vibrates.

Turn it up!

Right in front of the giant loudspeakers the volume might be well over 100 dB. No one is allowed to stand there.

3. Invisible ripples spread out as sound waves.

2. Diaphragm moves backwards and stretches air particles apart.

1. Diaphragm moves forwards and squashes air particles together.

volume loudness or intensity of a sound

Super-sonics

High in the clear blue sky, a jet plane roars overhead. Suddenly there's a massive boom, like a clap of thunder. But where's the storm?

The sound of thunder is made by the plane – it's called a **sonic** boom. It happens when jet planes go very fast. Waves of sound travel at about 1,230 kilometres per hour (764 miles per hour). If planes go faster than this, they squash the air in front of them so much and so fast that we hear a "BOOM".

At a massive fireworks display, you see the flashes before you hear the bangs. That's because light travels a million times faster than sound.

Sound words

"Supersonic" means faster than sound. But the speed of sound varies. Near the ground it's about 1,230 kilometres per hour (764 miles per hour). Very high up, where the air is cold and thin, it's 1,100 kilometres per hour (684 miles per hour).

sonic to do with sound

10

1. Zoom!
The plane goes faster than the speed of sound.

As the jet speeds up, it leaves its sound behind, so the pilot inside hears very little!

2. Squash!
Air cannot move out of the way quickly enough and piles up at the front.

3. Shock!
A cone of squeezed, high-**pressure** air spreads out as a shock wave.

4. Boom!
People hear the shock wave as a sonic boom.

pressure   pushing or squeezing force

Monster grunter

A seagull bobs up and down on a quiet sea, but underwater, it's a very different story.

Under the sea there are lots of different noises, from ship propellers and whining speedboats to crashing waves. There are noisy animals like claw-clicking crabs and squeaking dolphins. But nothing matches the hums and wails of whales.

The world's largest, loudest animal is the blue whale. It is 30 metres (100 feet) long, weighs over 100 tonnes (110 tons) and its deep, rumbling grunt is louder than a space rocket!

*Scientists use **hydrophones** to hear underwater sounds like whales moaning, dolphins clicking and submarines cruising past. The humpback whale is one of the noisiest. Its basic song lasts 10–15 minutes, but it repeats this for 20 hours!*

hydrophones   microphones that detect sounds in water

At breeding time, male whales sing long, loud songs to attract females from far away in the sea.

Biggest grunt

The blue whale's grunt measures a truly earsplitting 188 dB. The loudest land animal is the howler monkey, at 140 dB.

The blue whale sings while holding its breath underwater by moving air around inside its head, throat and lungs.

The air vibrates the whale's body, sending sound waves in all directions.

The sounds travel hundreds of kilometres through the ocean.

13

Do ears split?

Have you ever heard someone say a noise is "earsplitting"? If a sound is too loud, ears really can split!

Sound vibrations pass from the eardrum along three tiny bones to a small snail-shaped part, the cochlea. This turns them into nerve signals for our brain.

The flap of skin we call our ear doesn't hear. It guides sounds into a dark, mysterious tunnel called the ear canal, which is about 2.5 centimetres (1 inch) long. The ear canal ends at our **eardrum**. Sound waves bounce off the eardrum and make it vibrate. The vibrations travel to the inner ear, where they are turned into **nerve signals**. The nerve signals are recognized as sounds by our brain.

Ear bones

Nerve to brain

Cochlea

Ear canal

Eardrum

eardrum   small, skin-like patch in the ear canal

Too-loud sounds or things poked into the ear can split, tear or rupture the eardrum.

Earsplitting sounds

- Sounds over 130 dB cause ear pain, warning of serious damage.

- Sounds above 160 dB tears or ruptures the eardrum.

The eardrum is the same size as your little fingernail.

Thin, delicate, skin-like material.

This eardrum has broken because of an ear infection.

Like skin, most eardrum tears gradually heal.

The ear bone called the hammer pokes out of the eardrum's torn edge.

nerve signals   tiny pulses of electricity moving along nerves, carrying information

Take off

Imagine standing next to a jet aeroplane as it takes off, its engine noise shaking the ground beneath you... This is what it's like on an aircraft carrier.

Loud music is great for dancing. But people exposed to very loud noises without ear protection sometimes don't notice as their hearing worsens ... until their ears are permanently damaged.

Working on an aircraft carrier is one of the world's noisiest jobs. People stay on the carrier deck as planes take off and land, in case of emergency. Of course, the deck crew wear **ear-defenders**. So do people in other noisy places, like factories, building sites and roadworks. Otherwise, hour after hour, day after day, their hearing would suffer.

ear-defenders   padded cups over the ears to keep out noise

Jet power

A jet fighter at take-off produces over 140 dB.
The pilot's helmet and **cockpit** protect his ears.

The carrier deck crew are well protected against engine noise, heat and fumes.

Gases roaring from the jet engines cause massive noise.

Special earphones in the helmet fit the ears closely to keep out most noise.

Deck space is limited so the crew are close to the plane.

A radio link in the helmet allows the crew person to hear instructions.

cockpit   the area of the plane where the pilot sits

3, 2, 1... Blast off!

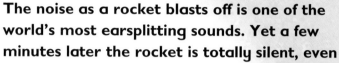

The noise as a rocket blasts off is one of the world's most earsplitting sounds. Yet a few minutes later the rocket is totally silent, even though its engine is still going and it's still moving. How?

People are kept several kilometres away when a space rocket is launched. Any nearer and the noise would be truly deafening as giant sound waves from the engine travel through the air. But when the rocket reaches space, there is no air for sound to move through, so it is silent. Without air, sound cannot be made – that's why everything in space is silent.

In space movie battles we often hear the noise of laser beams, guns and explosions. But in a real space battle, you'd only hear sounds inside your own spacecraft.

Rocket blast

A rocket's blast-off noise is up to 180 dB. The astronauts are protected from the noise because they are inside the spacecraft.

booster rockets bolt-on rockets for extra push at take-off, which then fall away

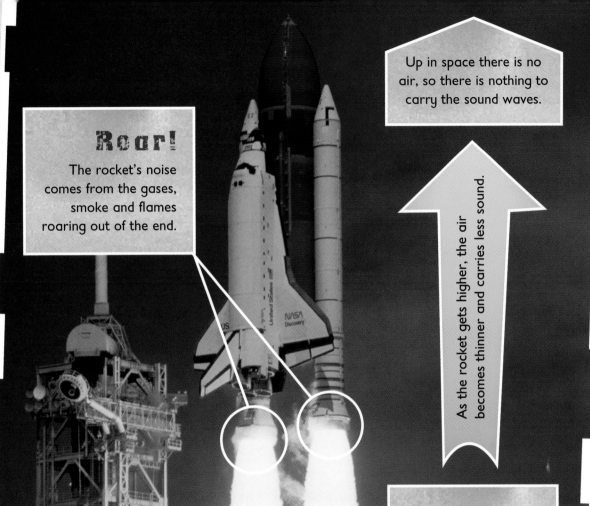

Roar!

The rocket's noise comes from the gases, smoke and flames roaring out of the end.

Up in space there is no air, so there is nothing to carry the sound waves.

As the rocket gets higher, the air becomes thinner and carries less sound.

Near the ground, the sound waves are carried through the air.

As the space shuttle lifts off, its two huge **booster rockets** make most of the noise.

Shout and scream!

Ever wanted to shout louder than the person beside you? Then you'll have to work on your vocal cords.

To speak, we use our **voicebox**, or larynx, in our neck. It has two stiff ridges called vocal cords on either side of an air passage coming up from the **windpipe**. To speak, muscles pull the vocal cords almost together, so they vibrate as air passes. When we shout, hum, sing, laugh or cry, sounds are made in the same way.

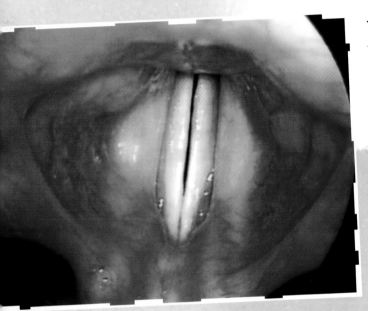

These vocal cords (white strips) are pulled together to speak. Shouting too loud for too long can hurt them and even cause small lumps, called nodules, which need medical treatment.

Shouting and burping

- **Some people can shout at over 130 dB.**
- **The world record for burping, where the noise comes from the stomach, is 118 dB.**

vocal cords stiff ridges inside the voicebox that make sounds

Footballing legend Ronaldo of Brazil celebrates another score.

3. Air passes the vocal cords and makes them vibrate.

4. The noise bounces around inside the throat, mouth and nose.

2. Air rushes up the windpipe and voicebox.

1. Chest muscles tighten to push out air fast.

Gooooaaaal!

5. The sound comes out of the mouth – and the nose too. Try pinching your nose shut as you speak!

windpipe tube below the voicebox, carrying air down to the lungs

Sonar power

One of the world's loudest machines is dark, sleek and sinister as it dips beneath the waves. Don't swim near a submarine when its sonar is on – it could blow up your ears!

A submarine's massive "pings" are even louder than a rocket taking off. They're part of the sonar, or **echo**-sounding equipment, which detects objects around the submarine. Why are the "pings" so loud? Because water's tiny particles are closer together, they bump into each other faster and more often. So sounds go further and faster in water than in air.

Echoes can only be heard when the object they bounce off, such as a cliff or wall, is at least 50 m (165 ft) away. Any closer and the echo merges with the original sound.

Loud and fast

- **Submarine sonar is incredibly loud – over 200 dB at just 1 metre (3 feet) away.**

- **Sounds in water travel at 5,400 kilometres per hour (3,300 miles per hour), over four times faster than in air.**

echo   to bounce sound off a hard surface

Ping!

Pings from the submarine's sonar travel out as sound wave beams.

Bounce!

The pings **reflect** (or echo) off objects nearby.

Listen

The sub's underwater microphones pick up the returning pings.

Locate

The direction and timing of the pings show the location of objects on the sonar screen.

reflect bounce off, as with light rays and sound waves

Jungle talk

Yum!

Eeek!

It's dusk in Africa. Elephants talk using deep rumbling sounds. Bats hunt with noisy squeaks. Zebras listen for a lion in the grass. Can you hear all this? No? That's normal for a human.

Many sounds are too low, too high or too faint for our ears. The deepest, lowest-**pitched** sounds we can hear are made by objects that vibrate slowly, 20 to 30 times each second. The number of vibrations per second is called the **frequency**. Our shrillest, highest-pitched sounds are made by much faster vibrations, up to 20,000 per second. Many animals make and hear much lower or higher sounds.

A bat's squeaks and clicks are too high for us to hear. They bounce off objects – like this doomed moth – and the bat works what's around it out from the echoes.

Low, high

- **Elephant rumbles measure up to 117 dB.**

- **Big bats aren't much quieter, at 110 dB. We can't hear either of them!**

pitch whether a sound is high or low

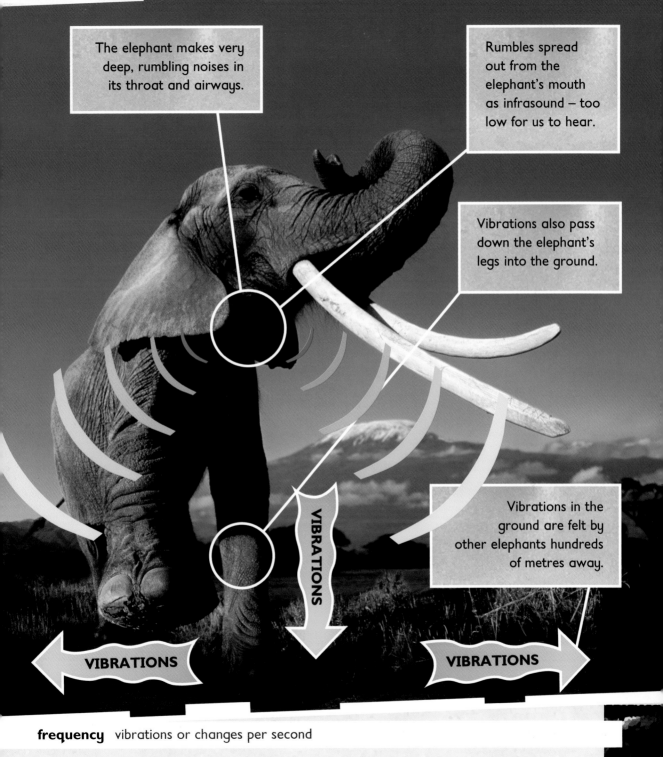

The elephant makes very deep, rumbling noises in its throat and airways.

Rumbles spread out from the elephant's mouth as infrasound — too low for us to hear.

Vibrations also pass down the elephant's legs into the ground.

Vibrations in the ground are felt by other elephants hundreds of metres away.

VIBRATIONS

VIBRATIONS

VIBRATIONS

frequency vibrations or changes per second

Smashing sound

Sound can smash things! Sound waves shake some objects so much that they fall apart. This can even be used to frighten away pirates!

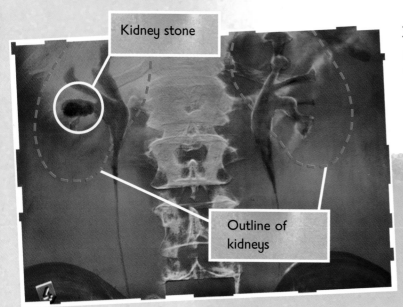

Kidney stone

Outline of kidneys

In 2005 off the coast of Africa, cruise ship *Seaborn Spirit* used a "sound cannon" to frighten away modern-day pirates. When sound waves hit something, they make it vibrate. Every object has its own natural speed of vibration, called its **resonance**. If this is the same as the sound waves, the object shakes more and more, out of control. It may shatter into pieces — even if it's a pirate!

In medicine, sound waves are beamed into the body to resonate and smash apart hard lumps called kidney or bladder stones. After breaking apart, the tiny pieces leave the body naturally.

Shattering sound

- **Windows shatter when they are hit by sounds of about 165 dB.**

- **Medical machines which break up kidney or bladder stones in the body are much safer, at 60–80 dB.**

resonance an object's natural vibrating or shaking speed

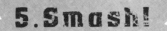

5. Smash!
Finally the glass shakes itself into bits.

4. Shudder!
More and more sound waves increase the shaking.

1. Strike!
Sound waves hit the glass and start it vibrating.

3. Shake!
The shaking gets more and more powerful.

2. Shiver!
The glass has the same natural resonance as the sound waves.

Too loud, shut it!

We love sounds like our friends talking, music, and birds singing. But traffic, machines, noisy neighbours and low-flying planes – shut it!

Too much noise is bad for us. Loud, unwanted sounds make us tense and irritated, and stop us from thinking clearly. They have other bad effects too. Really loud sounds don't just damage our hearing. They shake our eyeballs so we can't see, wobble our stomachs so we feel sick, and shudder parts deep in our ears that affect our balance, so we fall over.

Earphones and headphones might look cool and take you to music heaven. But if other people get annoyed by them, they're TOO LOUD!

Deafeningly loud

If you turn your music up too loud, for too long, you can damage your hearing. Long exposure to sounds, especially high-pitched sounds, over 85–90 dB, can cause damage. Even tiny earphones can make sounds of over 100 dB.

exposure to be left unprotected

In the recording studio, sound waves from separate instruments and voices are turned into electrical signals, which are then combined in the mixing desk.

The **recording studio** has soft, lumpy surfaces to soak up unwanted sound waves.

Microphone detects only sound waves coming directly from the singer, not sounds bouncing off the walls.

Sounds are controlled and changed by the knobs and sliders on the mixing desk.

recording studio a place where music and other sounds are recorded

Glossary

booster rockets bolt-on rockets for extra push at take-off, which then fall away

cockpit the area of the plane where the pilot sits

decibels unit used to measure sound's loudness or intensity

diaphragm cone-shaped part of a loudspeaker that makes sound waves

ear-defenders padded cups over the ears to keep out noise

eardrum small, skin-like patch in the ear canal

echo to bounce sound off a hard surface

exposure to be left unprotected

frequency vibrations or changes per second

hydrophones microphones that detect sounds in water

lava rock so hot it melts

nerve signals tiny pulses of electricity moving along nerves, carrying information

pitch whether a sound is high or low

pressure pushing or squeezing force

recording studio a place where music and other sounds are recorded

reflect bounce off, as with light rays and sound waves

resonance an object's natural vibrating or shaking speed

sonic to do with sound

source where something comes from

tsunamis huge waves set off by an earthquake or explosion

vibrate to shake quickly backwards and forwards

vocal cords stiff ridges inside the voicebox that make sounds

voicebox part in the neck that makes the sounds of the voice

volume loudness or intensity of a sound

windpipe tube below the voicebox, carrying air down to the lungs

Further information

Books

Essential Science: Changing Sounds by Peter Riley (Watts, 2006)
Essential facts about sound with experiments.

Horrible Science: Sounds Dreadful by Nick Arnold (Scholastic, 2008)
Fun, jokes, horribleness and some sound science.

The Hunchback of Notre Dame: Disney Edition by Victor Hugo (Ravette, 1996)
An exciting but tragic tale of love, mistaken identity, riots, theft, murder ... and deafness. Quasimodo the Hunchback has become deaf from ringing the giant bells of Notre Dame Cathedral, Paris.

Science Investigations: Sound by Jack Challoner (Hodder Wayland, 2006)
Straighforward explanations about the science of sound and acoustics.

Websites

www.santapod.co.uk/
The site of Santa Pod Raceway, home of British and European dragster racing, which calls itself "the fastest and loudest motorsport on earth".

www.howstuffworks.com/question124.htm
www.howstuffworks.com/hearing.htm
Two sites – one about decibels and measuring sound, and the other about how your ears work.

www.exploratorium.edu/theworld/sonar/sonar.html
How sonar works with whales and submarines.

www.pacdv.com/sounds/index.html
One of several online sources of free sounds, sound clips and SFX (sound effects).

www.deafplanet.com/en/deafplanet/
A fun, interactive website using ASL, American Sign Language, for people with hearing difficulties.

www.hse.gov.uk/noise/
Advice and guidelines about noise and hearing protection from the UK government's health and safety organization.

Films

Krakatoa: The Last Days directed by Sam Miller (BBC, 2006)
How the most earsplitting, earth-shattering event of recent history wreaked havoc for thousands of kilometres.

The Sound of Music directed by Robert Wise (20th Century Fox, 1965)
One of the most famous films ever, about how sounds and music can affect people's lives, and why some sounds are musical and pleasant while others are not.

Index